SCIENCE EXPLORER

JUNIOR

JUNIOR SCIENTISTS

Experiment with Liquids

by Matt Mullins

CHERRY LAKE PUBLISHING · ANN ARBOR, MICHIGAN

CHERRY
LAKE
Publishing

Published in the United States of America by Cherry Lake Publishing
Ann Arbor, Michigan
www.cherrylakepublishing.com

Content Editor: Robert Wolffe, EdD, Professor of Teacher Education, Bradley University, Peoria, Illinois
Reading Adviser: Cecilia Minden-Cupp, PhD, Literacy Consultant

Design and Illustration: The Design Lab

Photo Credits: Page 11, ©iStockphoto.com/Maica; page 15, ©amahuron/Shutterstock, Inc.; page 16, ©Andi Berger/Shutterstock, Inc.; page 23, ©Dmitry Rukhlenko/Shutterstock, Inc.; page 27, ©Studio 1One/Shutterstock, Inc.; page 28, ©Rob Marmion/Shutterstock, Inc.

Library of Congress Cataloging-in-Publication Data
Mullins, Matt.
  Junior scientists. Experiment with liquids / by Matt Mullins.
      p. cm.—(Science explorer junior)
  Includes bibliographical references and index.
  ISBN-13: 978-1-60279-846-5 (lib. bdg.)
  ISBN-10: 1-60279-846-X (lib. bdg.)
  1. Liquids—Experiments—Juvenile literature. 2. Science Projects—Juvenile literature. I. Title. II. Title: Experiment with liquids. III. Series.
  QC145.24.M85 2010
  532.0078—dc22   2009048840

Portions of the text have previously appeared in *Super Cool Science Experiments: States of Matter* published by Cherry Lake Publishing.

Cherry Lake Publishing would like to acknowledge the work of The Partnership for 21st Century Skills. Please visit *www.21stcenturyskills.org* for more information.

Printed in the United States of America
Corporate Graphics Inc.
July 2010
CLFA07

TABLE OF CONTENTS

Let's Experiment!

Experiments are fun!

Have you ever done a science **experiment**? They can be lots of fun! You can use experiments to learn about almost anything.

Good scientists observe the world around them.

This book will help you learn how to think like a scientist. Scientists have a special way of learning new things. Some people call it the Scientific Method. This is how it often works:

- Scientists notice things. They **observe** the world around them. They ask questions about things they see, hear, taste, touch, or smell. They come up with problems they would like to solve.

A scientist guesses what the answer to her question might be.

- They gather information. They use what they already know to guess the answers to their questions. This kind of guess is called a **hypothesis**.

- Then they test their ideas. They perform experiments or build models. They watch and write down what happens. They learn from each new test.

Scientists perform experiments to answer their questions.

- They think about what they learned and reach a **conclusion**. This means they come up with an answer to their question. Sometimes they **conclude** that they need to do more experiments!

When a scientist figures out the answer to her question, she has reached a conclusion.

Conclusion

What liquids do you use every day?

We will think like scientists to learn more about liquids. You see many different liquids every day. You shower with water. Water is a liquid. The juice you drink for breakfast is also a liquid. Have you ever wondered what makes something a liquid? How are some liquids different from others? We can do experiments to find the answers to these questions. Are you ready to be a scientist?

Making Changes

Three states of matter are gases, liquids, and solids.

What do we already know about liquids? A liquid is one of the states of matter. Two other states of matter are solids and gases. Are they connected in some way? Do you think we can turn a liquid into a solid? Let's experiment and find out!

First, choose a hypothesis:

1. L̶i̶q̶u̶i̶d̶s̶ ̶c̶a̶n̶ ̶b̶e̶ ̶t̶u̶r̶n̶ed into solids.
2. ̶ ̶ ̶ ̶ ̶ ̶ ̶ ̶ ̶ ̶ ̶ned into solids.

Let

ce be
olid?

Here's what you'll need:

- Water
- Orange juice
- Milk
- 3 ice cube trays
- A freezer
- Toothpicks

The kitchen is a good place to work.

Instructions:

1. Fill one ice cube tray with water.
2. Fill another tray with orange juice.
3. Fill the last tray with milk.

4. Put the three trays in the freezer.

5. Check the trays every 30 minutes for the next 4 hours. Use toothpicks to test if the liquids have turned solid. What do you notice? Write down what you see.

Put the three trays in the freezer.

Conclusion:

What happened to your liquids? You should have noticed that they have all frozen into solids! Did some of them take longer to freeze? Did you notice that the milk and the orange juice took longer to freeze? All liquids can freeze and turn solid if they get cold enough. Some need to be colder than others, though. Was your hypothesis correct?

You can enjoy a frozen treat on a hot day!

Density and Weight

These weights are heavy.

Solids, liquids, and gases all have weight. They also have **density**. Density is a **measurement** of how much something weighs compared to its size. A paperweight is very dense. It is small and heavy. Pillows are big and light. They are not very dense.

Different liquids have different densities. Let's compare three common liquids. We'll use rubbing alcohol, water, and vegetable oil. Which one do you think is the densest? Start by choosing a hypothesis:

1. Rubbing alcohol is the densest of the three liquids.
2. Water is the densest of the three liquids.
3. Vegetable oil is the densest of the three liquids.

Let's get started!

Vegetable oil is the densest of the three liquids.

Write down your hypothesis.

Here's what you'll need:

- An adult helper
- Glass jar
- ½ cup rubbing alcohol
- Blue and red food coloring
- Plastic spoon
- Funnel with a long tip
- ½ cup vegetable oil
- Drinking glass
- ½ cup water

Collect your supplies.

Instructions:

1. Pour the rubbing alcohol into the jar.
2. Add several drops of blue food coloring to the alcohol. Stir it with the spoon. You now have a blue liquid in the jar.
3. Put the funnel over the opening of the jar. The tip of the funnel should be long enough to reach down toward the bottom of the jar.

Put the funnel into the top of the jar.

Slowly pour the vegetable oil into the jar.

4. Slowly pour the vegetable oil into the funnel. Remove the funnel. Which liquid is on top? Which is on the bottom?

5. Add red food coloring to the water. Stir it to make a red liquid.

6. Slowly pour the red water into the jar through the funnel.

Conclusion:

Observe the layers of liquid. Do you see three bands of liquid? Which liquid is on top? Which one is on the bottom? Which one is in the center? The one on the bottom is the densest. It is heavier than the other two. The one on top is the least dense. Did you prove your hypothesis?

Which liquid is on top and which is on the bottom?

Connect the Drops

Have you ever broken your pencil?

Have you ever broken the tip of your pencil while you are writing? Have you ever torn a sheet of paper in half? Solid items like these cannot be put back together after they are broken apart. Do you think liquids work the same way? An experiment can answer that question!

Let's make a hypothesis:

1. Liquids can be put back together after they are pulled apart.
2. Liquids cannot be put back together after they are pulled apart.

Let's get started!

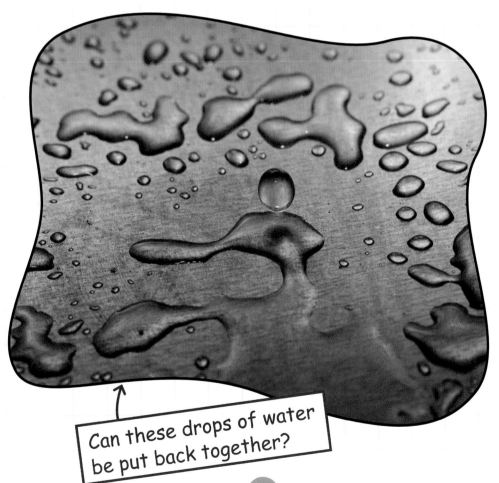

Can these drops of water be put back together?

Here's what you'll need:

- Water
- An eye dropper
- A straw
- A toothpick
- A flat surface

A countertop is a good flat surface to work on.

Instructions:

1. Use the eye dropper to place some large drops of water on a flat surface.
2. Use the toothpick to break the drops into smaller drops.

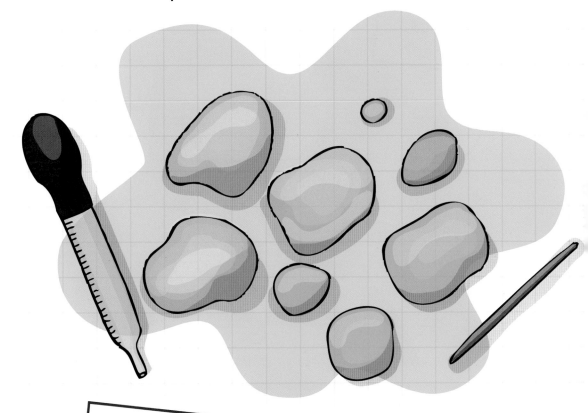

Use the toothpick to split up the water drops into smaller drops.

3. Try using the straw to blow the drops back together. Do they stick? Can you make them back into larger drops?

Are you able to blow the drops back together?

Conclusion:

You should have been able to put the drops of water back together. This is one of the things that makes liquids so different from solids. Solids have certain shapes. Liquids can change shape. They can be put back together. Did you prove your hypothesis?

You can swim in a liquid, but not in a solid.

Do It Yourself!

What will your next experiment be?

Okay, scientists! Now you know many new things about liquids. You learned that liquids can be turned into solids. You also learned that some liquids are denser than others. Finally, you learned that liquids can be put back together if they are broken apart. You learned these things by thinking like a scientist.

Do you have new questions about liquids? Maybe you are wondering if a liquid can be turned into a gas. You might want to test more liquids to see how long it takes for them to become solids. Why not use scientific thinking skills to answer your questions?

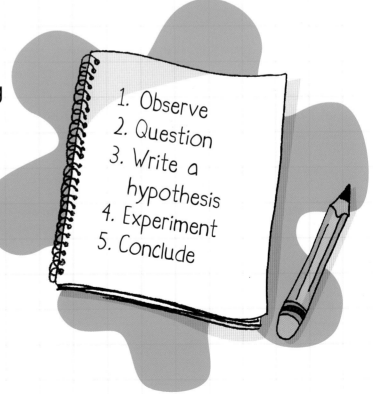

1. Observe
2. Question
3. Write a hypothesis
4. Experiment
5. Conclude

GLOSSARY

conclude (kuhn-KLOOD) to make a final decision based on what you know

conclusion (kuhn-KLOO-zhuhn) a final decision, thought, or opinion

density (DEN-sih-tee) a measurement of how much something weighs compared to its size

experiment (ecks-PARE-uh-ment) a scientific way to test a guess about something

hypothesis (hy-POTH-uh-sihss) a guess about what will happen in an experiment

measurement (MEH-zhur-muhnt) a number that describes an amount of something

method (METH-uhd) a way of doing something

observe (ob-ZURV) to see something or notice things by using the other senses

states of matter (STAYTZ UHV MAT-uhr) the different forms matter can take; for example, water can be a solid (ice), a liquid (drinking water), or a gas (steam)

FOR MORE INFORMATION

BOOKS

Claybourne, Anna. *The Science of a Glass of Water: The Science of States of Matter*. Pleasantville, NY: Gareth Stevens Publishing, 2008.

Gardner, Robert. *Melting, Freezing, and Boiling Science Projects with Matter*. Berkeley Heights, NJ: Enslow Elementary, 2006.

WEB SITES

CHEM4KIDS.COM
www.chem4kids.com/files/matter_intro.html
Learn more about the states of matter.

neoK12: States of Matter
www.neok12.com/States-of-Matter.htm
Play quiz games and watch videos about states of matter.

INDEX

ABOUT THE AUTHOR

Matt Mullins holds a master's degree in the history of science. He lives in Madison, Wisconsin, and writes about science, technology, and other topics that interest him.